Fun Ways to Learn the Whole Story of Jesus and His Love

Jesus' Last Week

Creative Bible-Learning Activities for Children Ages 6-12

Copyright ©1991 by Tracy Leffingwell Harrast. Published by David C. Cook Publishing Co.
Printed in the United States of America.

All puzzles and Bible activities are based on the NIV.

Scripture taken from the Holy Bible, New International Version, Copyright © 1973,
1978, 1984 International Bible Society.
Used by permission of Zondervan Bible Publishers.

Book Design by Tabb Associates
Cover Illustration by Gary Locke
Interior Illustrations by Anne Kennedy

THIS BOOK BELONGS TO:

_____

To My Children and Others Who Read This Book

Many of the events in Jesus' last week on earth were very sad, especially His death. But the story has a happy ending: Jesus is alive and we can live with Him forever! Please trust Him as the only way to go to heaven and follow Him all of your life.

—Tracy L. Harrast

Jesus' Last Week

CONTENTS

Jerusalem, Where Jesus Spent His Last Days

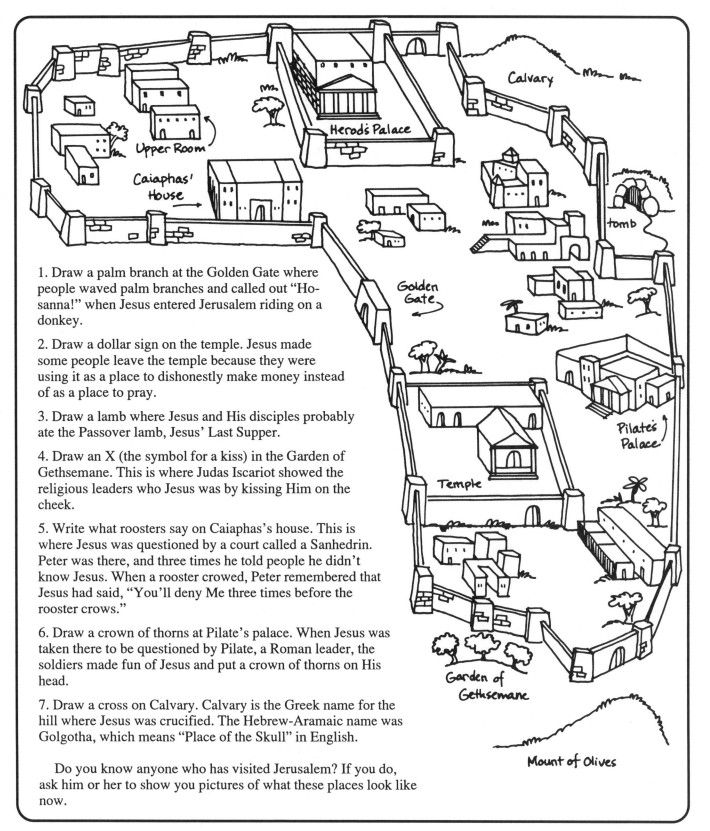

1. Draw a palm branch at the Golden Gate where people waved palm branches and called out "Hosanna!" when Jesus entered Jerusalem riding on a donkey.

2. Draw a dollar sign on the temple. Jesus made some people leave the temple because they were using it as a place to dishonestly make money instead of as a place to pray.

3. Draw a lamb where Jesus and His disciples probably ate the Passover lamb, Jesus' Last Supper.

4. Draw an X (the symbol for a kiss) in the Garden of Gethsemane. This is where Judas Iscariot showed the religious leaders who Jesus was by kissing Him on the cheek.

5. Write what roosters say on Caiaphas's house. This is where Jesus was questioned by a court called a Sanhedrin. Peter was there, and three times he told people he didn't know Jesus. When a rooster crowed, Peter remembered that Jesus had said, "You'll deny Me three times before the rooster crows."

6. Draw a crown of thorns at Pilate's palace. When Jesus was taken there to be questioned by Pilate, a Roman leader, the soldiers made fun of Jesus and put a crown of thorns on His head.

7. Draw a cross on Calvary. Calvary is the Greek name for the hill where Jesus was crucified. The Hebrew-Aramaic name was Golgotha, which means "Place of the Skull" in English.

Do you know anyone who has visited Jerusalem? If you do, ask him or her to show you pictures of what these places look like now.

Do You Know About Us?

Do you know the answers to these questions? If you don't know them yet, try again after you have read this book.

1.  What did people do with us to welcome Jesus into Jerusalem?

2. What did Judas do for thirty of us?

3. 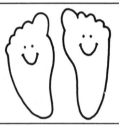 What did Jesus do to us at the Last Supper?

4. What did Jesus say you should think of when you eat and drink us?

5.  What did Peter tell people three times before I crowed?

6. Why was I empty?

The Disciples Find a Donkey

On His way to Jerusalem, Jesus stopped near Bethphage and Bethany at a hill called the Mount of Olives. He sent two of His disciples to a small village saying, "As you enter it, you will find a colt tied there which no one has ever ridden. Untie it and bring it here. If anyone asks you, 'Why are you doing this?' tell him, 'The Lord needs it and will send it back here shortly.'"

When the disciples entered the village, they saw a donkey in the street, tied in a doorway. The donkey's owners asked the disciples why they were untying it. The disciples said what Jesus had told them to say, and the owners let them take the donkey.

The disciples brought the donkey to Jesus, threw their cloaks on it, and helped Jesus get onto it so He could ride into Jerusalem.

Make a Potato Donkey

What You Need

- 2 potatoes (1 medium, 1 small)
- 6 Popsicle sticks
- black marker
- brown or black yarn
- scissors
- glue
- small doll clothes (these can be made by cutting and stapling scraps of fabric)

What You Do

1. Poke four Popsicle sticks into the large potato for legs.
2. Poke two Popsicle sticks through the small potato for ears on the top and a neck on the bottom.
3. Poke the neck sticks into the large potato, too.
4. Now you can make your donkey "come alive." Draw eyes and a smile with the marker. Cut small pieces of yarn and glue them on the potatoes for a mane and a tail.
5. When the glue has dried, drape doll clothes over the donkey the way the disciples draped their cloaks over the donkey that Jesus rode.

Draw a star in this box when you've read Matthew 21:1-7; Mark 11:1-7; and Luke 19:28-35.

Jesus Rides into Jerusalem

In Bible times, kings rode horses in battle and donkeys during times of peace. Jesus entered Jerusalem riding a donkey to show that He was a peaceful king. Sometimes people call this "The Triumphal Entry."

Many people were there to see Jesus, and they laid their coats and palm branches in the road. That was how they celebrated when a king came.

People were very excited and praised God for the miracles they had seen Jesus do. They shouted, "Hosanna! Blessed is he who comes in the name of the Lord! Blessed is the coming kingdom of our father David! Hosanna in the highest!"

When the other people in the city heard the noise, they asked who it was. The crowds told them "This is Jesus, the prophet from Nazareth in Galilee."

Some of the Jewish leaders thought that the people were getting a little carried away, and they told Jesus to make them settle down. Jesus said, "I tell you, if they keep quiet, the stones will cry out."

The people were very excited, but when Jesus saw Jerusalem ahead, He cried. He knew that the city would be destroyed by their enemies. The people didn't realize that Jesus was God and that accepting Him would have brought them peace.

Help Jesus get to Jerusalem by guiding Him through this maze.

Draw a star in this box when you've read Matthew 21:8-11; Mark 11:8-10; and Luke 19:36-44.

Hosanna!

As Jesus entered Jerusalem, the people shouted, "Hosanna!" This word means "Save us!" Jesus came to save them and us from our sins so that we can live with God in heaven. If you want Him to be your Savior (to save you), you can ask Him right now.

Write 'Hosanna!' with Colored Spaghetti

What You Need

- cooked spaghetti noodles (cooled off with cold water and then drained)
- 4 bowls or paper cups
- food coloring
- spoon
- vegetable oil

What You Do

1. Divide the spaghetti into the cups or bowls. Put two drops of food coloring in each cup. Stir the noodles until they are evenly colored. Rinse off the extra food coloring.
2. Add a drop or two of oil to each cup and stir it into the noodles.
3. Write the words "Hosanna! (save us)" with the noodles on a piece of paper. (They will stick to it without glue.)
4. Decorate the rest of the page. (NOTE: The noodles will shrink as they dry; the fun of this project is making it, not keeping it.)

When you've finished your picture, thank God for sending Jesus who saves us from our sins!

Wave a Palm Branch

In Bible times, people gave a king honor by waving palm branches and laying them in his path as he entered the city. Many of the people in Jerusalem were very happy when they saw Jesus riding like a king on a donkey. They waved palm branches, laid them in Jesus' path, and called "Hosanna!" which meant "Save us!"

Make a Palm Branch

What You Need

- four sheets of paper (typing paper, construction paper, or newspaper)
- scissors
- tape

1

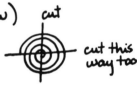

2

cut

cut again

(top view)

cut

cut this way too

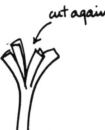

3

Pull from center

Hosanna!

What You Do

1. Roll one sheet of paper into a tube. When the first sheet is almost rolled up, tuck in another sheet of paper and keep rolling. Continue until all of the sheets are rolled.
2. Cut a slit as shown. If the paper is too thick for you to cut it, you can ask a grown-up for help. Turn the tube and cut another slit as shown.
3. Reach inside the tube and pull up the center. Now you have a palm branch! Tape the bottom so it doesn't unwind.

You can pretend that you were in Jerusalem when Jesus came riding in on a donkey. Wave your palm branch and shout "Hosanna!"

Jesus Clears the Temple

Think you can only find action, excitement, and adventure at the movies? Think again! The Bible is full of action! *Cross out every Q and Z from this story and you'll find a tale of toppling tables and much more!*

Thqe temzple wzas Goqd'sz hzoquse. Itz wasq supzposqed toz beq qaz zholy placez, bzut theq peoqple werzen't treaqting qit thaqt wzay. Thqey szold qanimals (szuch qas dozves) forq sacrizfices qat zhigh qprices thezre. Monqey zchazngers werqe therze charzging wzay tooq muzch. Thqey exchangezd forezign moqnezy forq mzoneqy thazt qwas zused qin Jerzusaqlem soz peoqple couqld buzy zaniqmals forz sacqrifzices.

Jesusz sqaid, "qIt zis wriqtten, 'Mzy hozuse qwill bez qcalled qa zhouqse zof praqyerz,' zbuqt yoqu hazve mazde qit za 'dzen qof thiezves.'" Hez chzased thze pezopleq wzho wezre buyizng aqnd sellizng zout ofz theq temzple. Hze turqned ovzer theq tables oqf the monqey chaqngers and the beqnches of the peqople seqlling pigzeons. Jesusq woulzdn't lezt anzyone comze qin bringinzg thinzgs toq sezll.

Evqzery daqzy zafqter thzat, Jzesus taugzht zaqt tzhe tezmpqle. Peozple whqo coulzdn't waqlk qor szee caqme tzo Jesus andz Heq hezaled theqm. Childzren qin zthe tempqle arzea shouqted, "Hozsanna tqo tzhe Son of Dzavid." Thze Jewiqsh chuzrch leadqers wanqted tzo kizll zJesus beqcause zthey wezre zafraiqd pezopleq wqould qfolzlow Hiqm zinsqtead qof thezm.

☐ *Draw a star in this box when you've read Matthew 21:12-16; Mark 11:15-18; and Luke 19:45-48.*

Mary Anoints Jesus

*To decode the **bold** words, change each letter to the letter that
follows it in the alphabet. Change Z to A.*

Jesus was 1. **dzshmf** _____ dinner at Simon the Leper's
2. **gntrd** _____ in Bethany. Lazarus (whom Jesus raised from the
3. **cdzc**) _____ and others were eating with 4. **Idrtr** _____.
Lazarus's sister Martha was serving the 5. **ldzk** ____. Lazarus's
other sister Mary came in with a 6. **vghsd** _____ stone jar of
perfume that was so expensive it 7. **vntkc** _____ take almost a
year to earn enough 8. **lnmdx** _____ to buy it.

Mary did something very 9. **knuhmf** _____: she poured the
perfumed 10. **nhk** ___ on Jesus' head. This was called *anointing,*
and it was done to 11. **oqnogdsr** _____, priests, and 12.
jhmfr _____ . Mary also poured some oil on Jesus' feet and
wiped them with her 13. **gzhq** _____. Jesus said this was like
preparing 14. **Ghl** ____ for burial.

Judas Iscariot and 15. **nsgdqr** _____ criticized Mary and said
she was being 16. **vzrsdetk** _____ . Jesus said that what she
did was good. He said, "Wherever the 17. **fnrodk** _____ is
preached throughout the world, what 18. **rgd** ____ has done will
also be told, in 19. **ldlnqx** _____ of her."

Something to Think About

Mary's perfumed oil was probably the most expensive thing she owned.
It cost so much that it would have taken almost a full year for someone to
earn that much money. Today it would probably cost more than some cars.
She used the oil to anoint Jesus because she loved Him very deeply and
honored Him as her king. Do you love Jesus as much as Mary did? Is He
more important to you than anything else in your life?

Draw a star in this box when you've read Matthew 26:6-13; Mark 14:3-9; and John 12:1-11.

Make Perfumed Oil

Give it to someone you love the way Mary did.

What You Need

- clean baby food jar or other glass jar with lid
- 1/4 cup baby oil
- potpourri
- piece of sterile gauze or cheesecloth
- small, decorated bottle

What You Do

1. Pour the baby oil and potpourri into the glass jar and screw on the lid.

2. Leave the jar on a sunny windowsill for 2-3 full days.

3. Remove the lid and cover the top of the jar with the gauze or cheesecloth.

4. Strain the potpourri out of the perfume by pouring it through the gauze or cheese-cloth into the decorated bottle. If its scent isn't strong enough, pour it back into the glass jar and repeat the instructions using new potpourri.

5. Put the top on the bottle and give it to a friend.

Judas Betrays Jesus

Put these words where they belong in the story: Supper, silver, born, thirty, killed, better, dipped, himself, Garden, kissed

Judas Iscariot helped the religious leaders catch Jesus so they could have Him 1._____. Judas went to them and asked them what they would give him for helping them get Jesus. They promised him 2._____ pieces of 3._____.

Jesus knew all about this and told the disciples at the Last 4._____ "One of you will betray me." The disciples were very sad and each asked, "Surely not I, Lord?" Jesus said it was the person who 5._____ his bread into a bowl the same time He did. Jesus said that things would go the way the prophets of the Old Testament had written that they would, but it would have been 6._____ for the man who betrayed Him never to have been 7._____. When Judas asked if it was him, Jesus said, "Yes, it is you." Then Jesus told him to do quickly what he needed to do. Judas left and went to the religious leaders.

Jesus knew that Judas was bringing a crowd to catch Him in the 8._____ of Gethsemane. He could have escaped, but He didn't. Judas had told the religious leaders, "The one I kiss is the man; arrest him." So Judas 9._____ Jesus when he found Him, and the people took Jesus away.

Afterward Judas Iscariot killed 10._____.

Draw a star in this box when you've read Matthew 26:14-16, 21-25, 45-56; 27:3-10; Mark 14:10, 11, 18-21, 41-50; Luke 22:3-6, 21-23, 47, 48; John 13:21-30; and 18:1-12.

The Passover

Passover was a holy day that Jewish people celebrated each year. It helped them remember a night in Old Testament times when death passed over the homes of the people who had put lambs' blood on their door frames. The firstborn in homes without blood on their door frames died.

When the disciples asked Jesus where He wanted them to prepare the Passover meal, Jesus said, "Go into the city, and a man carrying a jar of water will meet you. Follow him. Say to the owner of the house he enters, 'The teacher asks: Where is my guest room, where I may eat the Passover with my disciples?' He will show you a large upper room, furnished and ready. Make preparations for us there." The disciples went into the city and found just what Jesus had described, so they prepared the Passover meal.

Draw a  Step-by-Step

You can draw your own lamb to help you remember that Jesus is our Passover lamb!

How to Draw a Lamb: *Practice Drawing Here:*

1. *Draw a face.*

2. *Draw fleece.*

3. *Draw an ear.*

4. *Draw legs.*

Draw a star in this box when you've read Matthew 26:17-19; Mark 14:12-16; Luke 22:7-13; and I Corinthians 5:7.

Washing Feet

Jesus news-spaper it was 🕐 4 Him 2 🚦 2 heaven, and He wanted 2 show His 12 👥 how much He ♡ +ed them. As the Passover 🍽 was 🐝 +ing served, Jesus got ⬆ and wrapped a 🧣 around His waist. Then Jesus washed the 🦶 of the 12 👥 and dried them [OFF]. Peter didn't want Jesus 2 do such a hum+🐄 thing 4 him.

Jesus said, "Unless 👁 wash U, U have no part with 0-T." "Then, Lord, not just my 🦶 but my ✋ and 🗣 as well!" Peter said.

Jesus said, "A 🧍 who has had a 🛁 needs only 2 wash his 🦶; his whole body is clean. And U R clean, though ⟋ every 1 of U." Jesus said not every 1 there was clean 🐝+ cause He news-spaper that Judas Iscariot 📌 betray Him.

When Jesus finished washing their 🦶, Jesus returned 2 His place at the 🍽. Jesus said, " 👁 , your Lord and Teacher, have washed your 🦶, U also should wash 1 another's 🦶. 👁 have set you an example that U should do as 👁 have done 4 U. 👁 tell U the truth, no servant is > his master, nor is a messenger > the 1 who sent him. Now that U 👃 -se these things, U will 🐝 blessed if U do them."

Draw a star in this box when you've read John 13:1-17.

Make Footprints

Did you know that you can make a stamp that looks like a footprint using your hand? Here's how you can make mysterious cards to leave when you've secretly served others.

What You Need

- 3" x 5" index cards (without lines)
- ink pad or jar lid with paint

What You Do

1. Make a fist with your hand and roll the side of your fist on the ink pad.
2. Press your inked hand on the 3" x 5" card.
3. Now you can add toes to the top of your foot by rolling your knuckles in the ink and then pressing them across the top of the foot. You can use a thumbprint for the big toe.
4. When you serve someone secretly, leave one of your footprints behind.
Optional—You can make your feet different colors by using different colors of ink or notecards. You can also write a message on your card such as "Serve one another in love. Galatians 5:13."

At the Last Supper

Decode what Jesus taught His disciples at the Last Supper, then memorize each of the verses. When you know them by heart, color in the heart at the beginning of each verse.

I know
John 14:2
by heart.

I know
John 14:6
by heart.

I know
John 14:12
by heart.

I know
John 14:18
by heart.

CODE

A = ♩ B = 🍓 C = 🍇 D = 📺 E = 🏢 F = 🛹 G = 🚃
H = 🚋 I = ～ J = 🚂 K = 🦀 L = 🌲 M = ▪ N = ▪
O = 𓂀 P = 🗡 Q = 🏢 R = 🏢 S = ✉ T = 🏢 U = 𓅃 V = ☥
W = 🏢 X = 🌷 Y = 🌷 Z = 🌷

I know John 14:23 by heart.

I know John 14:26 by heart.

I know John 14:27 by heart.

Draw a star in this box when you've read the verses listed above.

19

The Bread and the Cup

While Jesus and the disciples were eating the Last Supper, Jesus took the bread, thanked God for it, and gave it to His disciples. Jesus told them to eat it and said, "This is my body given for you; do this in remembrance of me."

Then He took the cup, thanked God for it and said, "Drink from it, all of you. This is my blood of the covenant [agreement between God and people], which is poured out for many for the forgiveness of sins. I tell you, I will not drink of this fruit of the vine from now on until that day when I drink it anew with you in my Father's kingdom."

Believers today still eat bread and drink wine or grape juice to remember Jesus' death for our sins. What is this called in your church? _____

Even though you weren't around back then, you can still have forgiveness. To find out what Jesus gave so we could be forgiven, cross out the letters that spell each picture.

BBROEDAYD

GBRALPEO JOUIDCE

Draw a star in this box when you've read Matthew 26:26-30; Mark 14:22-26; and Luke 22:14-20.

The Mount of Olives

After the Last Supper, Jesus and His disciples went to the Mount of Olives. (Judas Iscariot wasn't there because he had gone to tell the chief priests where they could find Jesus.) When they were on the Mount of Olives, Jesus told His disciples many things. *Look up the verses to discover what Jesus told His disciples and complete the puzzle.*

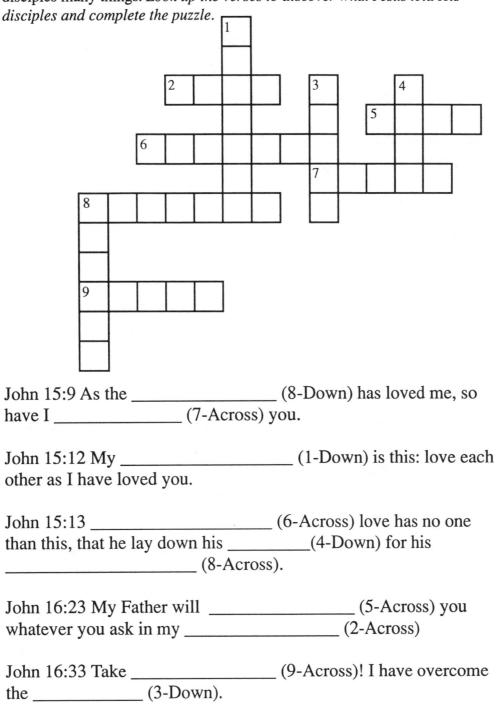

John 15:9 As the _____ (8-Down) has loved me, so have I _____ (7-Across) you.

John 15:12 My _____ (1-Down) is this: love each other as I have loved you.

John 15:13 _____ (6-Across) love has no one than this, that he lay down his _____(4-Down) for his _____ (8-Across).

John 16:23 My Father will _____ (5-Across) you whatever you ask in my _____ (2-Across)

John 16:33 Take _____ (9-Across)! I have overcome the _____ (3-Down).

Draw a star in this box when you've read John 15:9, 12, 13; 16:23, 33.

Prayer in the Garden

*To complete the story below, unscramble each **BOLD, CAPITALIZED** word.*

Jesus and His disciples went to a 1. **RAGNED** _____ called Gethsemane. Jesus told the disciples to sit in one place while He went to pray in another place. He took 2. **RTPEE** _____, James, and John with Him. Jesus began to feel very sad. He said that He was so sad He almost felt like He was dying. Then He told Peter, James, and John to wait while He prayed.

Then Jesus went a little 3. **RATERHF** _____ and prayed, "My Father, if it is possible, may this cup be taken from Me." Jesus was saying that if everyone could be saved from their sins without Him dying, He would like to stay alive and not suffer. Jesus also said, though, "Not as I will, but as you will." He wanted to do what God wanted Him to do. Then an 4. **NLEGA** _____ appeared and gave Him strength. But Jesus still felt terrible and prayed so deeply that He started to sweat. It was like big drops of 5. **LODOB** _____ that fell to the ground.

Jesus got up and went to His disciples, but they were 6. **LESAPE** _____. He said to Peter, "Could you men not keep watch with me for one 7. **ROHU** _____? Watch and pray so that you will not fall into temptation. The spirit is willing, but the body is weak."

Jesus went away a second time and 8. **REDPYA** _____, "My Father, if it is not possible for this cup to be taken away unless I drink it, may your will be done." Then He went and found the disciples asleep again.

He left them a third time and prayed the same thing. When He came back, He said to His disciples, "Are you still sleeping and 9. **STINGER** _____? Look, the hour is near, and the Son of Man is betrayed into the hands of 10. **NISRENS** _____." Then He said, "Rise, let us go! Here comes my betrayer!"

☐ *Draw a star in this box when you've read Matthew 26:36-46; Mark 14:32-42; and Luke 22:39-46.*

Jesus Is Arrested

Jesus didn't fight the men who came to arrest Him, but one of His disciples sure wanted to! *To find out what happened, read the story below, then find the ten underlined words from the story in the puzzle.*

Judas Iscariot knew that Jesus often went to the Garden of <u>Gethsemane</u>. Judas led a large crowd into the garden where Jesus had been praying. They carried <u>lanterns</u>, torches, swords, and <u>clubs</u>.

Judas had told the crowd ahead of time that he would kiss Jesus so they would know who He was. Jesus asked Judas, "Judas, are you betraying the Son of Man with a kiss?" Judas said, "Greetings, Rabbi," and <u>kissed</u> Him. The men grabbed Jesus and started taking Him away. Jesus told the men to let the disciples go.

Then Simon Peter pulled out a sword and cut off the right <u>ear</u> of the high priest's servant, Malchus. Jesus said, "No more of this!" and He touched Malchus's ear and healed it. Jesus told Simon Peter to put away his sword and said, "All who draw the sword will die by the sword. Do you think I cannot call on my <u>Father,</u> and he will at once put at my disposal more than twelve legions of <u>angels</u>? But how then would the Scriptures be fulfilled that say it must happen in this way?"

Jesus told the <u>crowd</u> that they were treating Him like a thief. He said "Every day I was with you in the temple courts, and you did not lay a hand on Me. But this is your hour—when <u>darkness</u> reigns." All of this happened the way the Old Testament prophets had said it would. Then the people tied up Jesus and the <u>disciples</u> ran away.

```
R B K J D W O R C G N B
K C L U B S N E F E S P
I B N A R A B T A T E H
S M O R V I N S T H L R
S L R O F N P Q H S P L
E B D L E A R T E E I O
D A R K N E S S R M C V
L O N G F B U T I A S H
J I E R C R O W D N I C
O L S R L B I C S E D W
S N R E T N A L I M A R
```

Draw a star in this box when you've read Matthew 26:47-56; Mark 14:43-52; Luke 22:47-53; and John 18:1-12.

Religious Leaders Question Jesus

Jesus didn't have a lawyer, but He was put on trial anyway. You can read about His trial in the story below. One letter is missing from some of the words in each line that has an empty box beside it. *Put the missing letter in the box beside the line as you read the story, and when you have finished reading the story, the letters will form a message.*

☐ _esus was taken from the Garden of Gethsemane to the home of Caiaphas, the Jewish high priest.

☐ Many l_ad_rs had gath_r_d tog_th_r to form a church court called a

☐ _anhedrin. They were were trying to find Je_u_ guilty of a crime _o He would be killed.

☐ The high priest asked Jes_s abo_t His disciples and teaching. Jes_s said, "I have spoken openly to the world.

☐ I alway_ taught in _ynagogue_ or at the temple, where all the people_ come together. I said nothing in secret. Why question Me? Ask those who heard me. Surely they know what I said."

☐ _hen Jesus said this, one of the men nearby hit Jesus in the face. The man

☐ said, "Is this the w_y you _nswer the high priest?"

☐ Je_u_ _aid, "If I _aid _omething wrong, te_tify a_ to what i_ wrong. But if I spoke the truth, why did you strike Me?"

The chief priests and Sanhedrin all tried to find ways to prove that Jesus

☐ should be killed. Ma_y people came as witnesses, but they lied and their

☐ st_ries didn't agree. Finally tw_ pe_ple said that Jesus said "I am able t_

☐ des_roy the _emple of God and rebuild i_ in _hree days." Caiaphas said _o Jesus, "Are you not going to answer this?"

Jesus remained silent.

☐ Caiaphas said, "Tell us if you are the Christ, the Son of _od."

☐ Jes_s said, "Yes, it is as yo_ say. B_t I say to all of yo_: In the f_t_re yo_

☐ w_ll see the Son of Man s_tt_ng at the r_ght hand of the Mighty One and coming on the clouds of heaven."

☐ Caiaphas said that Jesus had broken the Jewish _aw by c_aiming to be God's Son. The peop_e said Jesus deserved _o die.

☐ _hey hi_ Him wi_h _heir fis_s and spi_ in His face.

☐ The_ blindfolded Him, slapped Him, and said, "Prophes_ to us, Christ. Who hit you?"

☐ *Draw a star in this box when you've read Matthew 26:57-68; Mark 14:53-65; Luke 22:54, 63; and John 18:12-14, 19-24.*

Peter and the Rooster

Peter was one of Jesus' closest friends and followers, but after Jesus was arrested, Peter was afraid to tell people that he even knew Jesus. Jesus had told him earlier, "Tonight—before the rooster crows twice you yourself will disown me three times." Peter said that he would never do that.

Later that night while Jesus was being questioned, Peter was warming himself by a fire in the courtyard. A servant girl said to Peter, "You also were with Jesus of Galilee." Peter said, "I don't know what you're talking about."

Peter was afraid. He didn't want to be arrested, too. Peter moved around and went to the gateway. Another girl saw him there and said, "This fellow was with Jesus of Nazareth." Peter again said, "I don't know the man!"

A little later, others said to him, "Surely you are one of them, for your accent gives you away." Peter insisted, "I don't know the man!"

Right then a rooster crowed. Twice. Jesus turned and looked straight at Peter and Peter remembered what Jesus had said. Peter had just done exactly what he said he would *never* do. Peter was sad that he had not told the truth about knowing Jesus. He went outside and cried.

Color this picture of Peter and see if you can find the hidden rooster.

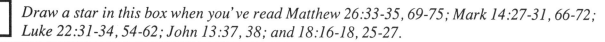

Draw a star in this box when you've read Matthew 26:33-35, 69-75; Mark 14:27-31, 66-72; Luke 22:31-34, 54-62; John 13:37, 38; and 18:16-18, 25-27.

Make a Rooster Puppet

When people excitedly and joyfully boast about something, it's called "crowing" about it. If you have asked Jesus to be your Savior, He has taken away your sins and made you able to live with God forever! Now that's *really* something to crow about! *Tell your friends that Jesus will do the same for them if they ask Him.*

Make this rooster puppet to tell Peter's story from the rooster's point of view.

What You Need

- a sheet of typing paper
- yellow and black markers
- scraps of red construction paper
- scissors
- glue or tape

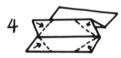

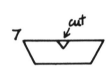

What You Do

1. *Fold over one corner of the typing paper as shown. Cut off the extra strip at the top and unfold your paper. It should be a square. (Make sure it is square. The puppet won't work if it isn't.)*

2. *Fold the square in half.*

3. *Fold each side back so that its edge touches the fold. (See illustration.)*

4. *Fold down the corners of the middle section. Fold up the corners of the side closest to you. Don't fold the corners of the far side.*

5. *Press together the sides that have their corners bent.*

6. *Now fold down the corners of the remaining side. Fold the last side in so that all of the sides are pressed together.*

7. *Cut a notch out of the middle of the longer top side that has two folded edges.*

8. *Fold out the four edges that are on the sides of the cutout notch.*

9. *Turn the puppet upside down. Put your thumb on point B and your middle finger on point A. (See illustration.) Bring your thumb and finger together, causing the puppet to close its mouth.*

10. *Now you can draw on eyes and color the beak yellow.*

11. *Cut the rooster's comb out of red construction paper, and glue or tape it to the puppet.*

Government Leaders Question Jesus

Read the story and then fit the underlined words into this puzzle.

The religious leaders took Jesus from the Jewish court to the palace of <u>Pilate</u>, a Roman leader. They said Jesus was claiming to be the king of the Jews. Jesus said His <u>kingdom</u> wasn't of this world.

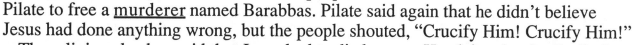

Pilate didn't quite know what to do with Jesus. Then Pilate heard that Jesus had started His ministry in Galilee, so he sent Jesus to Herod, the leader over Galilee. Herod asked Jesus lots of questions, but Jesus wouldn't answer, so Herod sent Him back to Pilate.

Pilate always released a prisoner at the Passover holiday. He asked the crowd if they wanted him to let Jesus go. The chief priests convinced the people to ask Pilate to free a <u>murderer</u> named Barabbas. Pilate said again that he didn't believe Jesus had done anything wrong, but the people shouted, "Crucify Him! Crucify Him!"

The religious leaders said that Jesus had to die because He claimed to be God's Son. This scared Pilate. Pilate asked Jesus where He came from, but Jesus didn't answer. Pilate said, "Do You refuse to speak to me? Don't You realize I have power either to free You or to crucify You?"

Jesus answered, "You would have no power over me if it were not given to you from above. Therefore the one who handed me over to you is guilty of a greater <u>sin</u>."

Pilate knew that Jesus really wasn't guilty, so he washed his hands in front of the people and said, "I am innocent of this man's blood. It is your responsibility!" Then Pilate freed Barabbas and sent Jesus to be crucified.

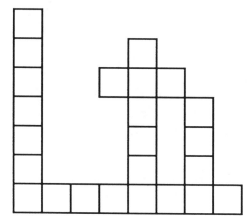

Pilate's soldiers took Jesus away. They took off His clothes and put a royal <u>robe</u> on Him. They put a crown of thorns on His head and made Him hold a stick as if it were a king's scepter. Then they kneeled in front of Him and teased, "Hail, king of the Jews!" The guards spit on Jesus and hit Him on His head again and again. Finally they took off the robe, put His own clothes on Him, and led Him away to crucify Him.

Draw a star in this box when you've read Matthew 27:11-31; Mark 15:1-15; Luke 22:66-71; 23:1-25; John 18:28-40; and 19:1-16.

Jesus Is Crucified

1. What was written on the sign?

3. What did one of the robbers ask Jesus?

2. What was one of the things Jesus prayed?

4. What was one of the lies the crowd said?

As the Roman soldiers were making Jesus carry His cross, they saw Simon from Cyrene and made him carry the cross for Jesus. There were many people following, and some of the were crying. Jesus said to them, "Do not weep for me; weep for yourselves and for your children." He said that things would be much worse for them and they would suffer much in the years ahead.

The soldiers brought Jesus to a place called Calvary or Golgotha, which means "The Place of the Skull." They nailed Jesus to the cross and crucified him between two criminals. Even when Jesus was dying on the cross, He still was full of love. He said, "Father, forgive them, for they do not know what they are doing." The soldiers offered Jesus wine with a drug in it that could ease His pain, but after He tasted it, He wouldn't drink it.

Then the soldiers gambled for His clothes. Prophets in Old Testament times had said they would do this. They also put a sign over His head that said: THIS IS JESUS, THE KING OF THE JEWS. The Jewish leaders wanted the sign to say that Jesus *said* He was the king of Jews, not that He really *was,* but Pilate said, "What I have written, I have written."

As people passed by Jesus, they yelled insults at Him and made fun of Him. Some said, "You who are going to destroy the temple and build it in three days, come down from the cross and save yourself!" Some of the chief priests said, "He saved others, but he can't save himself! Let this Christ, this King of Israel, come down now from the cross, that we may see and believe."

Two robbers were crucified with Jesus, one on each side. One of the men insulted Jesus. But the other robber said to him, "Don't you fear God since you are under the same sentence? We are punished justly, for we are getting what our deeds deserve. But this man has done nothing wrong." Then he said to Jesus, "Jesus, remember me when you come into your kingdom." Jesus answered, "I tell you the truth, today you will be with me in paradise."

Jesus' mother Mary, His aunt, another Mary (Clopas's wife), and Mary Magdalene were near Jesus' cross. Jesus saw His mother and His disciple John. He said to His mother, "Dear woman, here is your son," and to John, "Here is your mother." From that time on, John took care of Jesus' mother.

☐ *Draw a star in this box when you've read Matthew 27:32-44; Mark 15:21-32; Luke 23:26-43; and John 19:16-27.*

Jesus Dies

Put the giant letters from the numbered sentences in the blanks at the bottom of the page and you will find what the Roman leader and guards who crucified Jesus said.

1. From **N**oon until 3:00 in the afternoon the whole earth was dark.

2. At about 3:00 Jesus cried **O**ut in a loud voice, "Eloi, Eloi, lama sabachthani?" This meant, "My God, my God, why have you forsaken me?"

3. Some people thought that Jesus was callin**G** the Old Testament prophet Elijah.

4. When Jesus said, "I'm thirsty," someone **F**illed a sponge with wine vinegar, put it on a stick, and offered it to Jesus. Jesus took a drink and then said, "It is finished."

5. Jesus called out loudly, "Father, int**O** your hands I commit my spirit." Then He bowed His head and died.

6. At that moment the curtain in the temple that separate**D** people from God was torn in two from top to bottom.

7. There was an earthquake and rocks **S**plit.

8. Tombs broke **O**pen and many dead people who had loved God came back to life.

When the guards and Roman leader who were watching saw what happened, they were terrified and said, "Surely He was the

$$\overline{}\ \overline{}\ \overline{}\quad \overline{}\ \overline{}\quad \overline{}\ \overline{}\ \overline{}."$$
$$\ \ 7\ \ \ 5\ \ \ 1\quad\ \ 2\ \ \ 4\quad\ \ 3\ \ \ 8\ \ \ 6$$

Draw a star in this box when you've read Matthew 27:45-54; Mark 15:33-39; Luke 23:44-47; and John 19:28-30.

Jesus' Last Words

The Bible is so accurate and full of detail that it even tells us what Jesus said when He was up on the cross, just before He died. To find out what He said, move through the maze to the center cross.

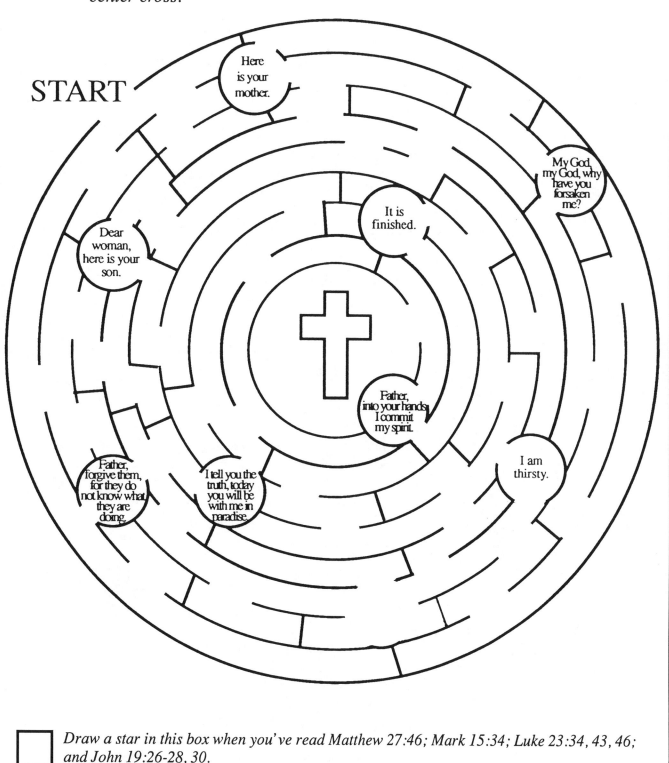

Draw a star in this box when you've read Matthew 27:46; Mark 15:34; Luke 23:34, 43, 46; and John 19:26-28, 30.

Make Simple Crosses

These crosses can be reminders of how much Jesus loves you. He died on the cross so you can go to heaven!

Cinnamon Cross

What You Need

- 1 tablespoon cinnamon
- 2 teaspoons white school glue
- bowl of water
- paper towel
- wax paper
- thin ribbon

What You Do

1. Mix the cinnamon and glue to form a sticky dough.
2. Shape the dough into a cross. If it starts to stick to your hands, wet them with a little bit of water.
3. Lay the cross on a piece of wax paper and draw a neat design in it with a toothpick.
4. When you've finished your design, poke a hole near the top with your toothpick.
5. When the cross is dry, string a thin ribbon through the hole and hang it up where it can remind you just how much Jesus loves you!

Dried Flower Cross

What You Need

- wildflowers
- wax paper
- heavy book
- clear Con-Tact paper
- scissors
- hole punch
- ribbon

What You Do

1. You can dry some wildflowers by laying them between pieces of wax paper and putting them between the pages of a heavy book. Leave them alone for at least a week.
2. When your flowers are ready, peel the backing off of a square of Con-Tact paper. Arrange your flowers in a cross shape on the sticky side of the Con-Tact paper. Press the sticky side of another square of Con-Tact paper on top. Be sure you smooth out any air bubbles.
3. Cut out your cross, leaving a border around the edges.
4. Now you can punch a hole in the top border and tie a ribbon in it. You can hang up your cross or use it as a bookmark.

Twig Cross

What You Need

- 2 twigs
- brown or black thread
- glue
- dried flowers

What You Do

1. Arrange the two twigs in a cross shape.
2. Carefully wrap the thread around the twigs very tightly so it makes an "X" where they meet. Wrap it around several times. Make a loop of thread in the back for hanging the cross.
3. Now you can decorate your cross by gluing dried flowers where the twigs meet.

Why Did Jesus Need to Die?

Jesus had a choice about whether to let people kill Him. At any time He could have called thousands of angels to help Him. Why did Jesus let the people crucify Him?

Each one of us has sinned. That sin makes us unable to go to heaven. There isn't anything we can do to get rid of our sins, and there isn't anything we can do that is good enough to make us deserve to go to heaven. God loves us though, and He wants us to live with Him in heaven. God loves us so much, in fact, that He sent the solution to our problem—Jesus!

Jesus chose to take the punishment we deserved for the wrong things we have done. If we really believe that God raised Jesus from the dead, and we say that Jesus is who the Bible says He is, we will be saved from the punishment for our sins. The only way we can be forgiven and live forever with God is through believing in Jesus.

Do you believe in Jesus? If you have not accepted Him as your Savior and Lord yet, you can do that now by praying a prayer like this in your own words:

Dear God,

Thank You for sending Jesus to take the punishment I deserve for the wrong things I have done. I believe You raised Him from the dead. I want to follow Him as my Lord all of my life.

In Jesus' name. Amen.

Color the picture using this code: 1=blue, 2=red, 3=yellow, 4=peach, 5=green, 6=purple, 7=pink

Draw a star in this box when you've read John 3:16, 23; John 14:6; Romans 3:23; and 10:9.

Jesus Is Buried

To find out what happened after Jesus died, match each statement below with the picture that fills its blank.

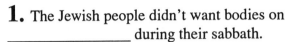

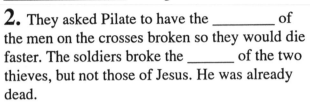

1. The Jewish people didn't want bodies on _____ during their sabbath.

2. They asked Pilate to have the _____ of the men on the crosses broken so they would die faster. The soldiers broke the _____ of the two thieves, but not those of Jesus. He was already dead.

3. When the soldiers saw that Jesus was already dead, they pierced His side with a _____.

4. A rich man named Joseph of Arimathea, one of Jesus' followers, asked Pilate for Jesus' body. Joseph and Nicodemus took Jesus' body and wrapped it with strips of clean linen _____ and seventy-five pounds of spices.

5. After Joseph and Nicodemus had wrapped Jesus' body, they placed it in a _____ that Joseph had bought for himself.

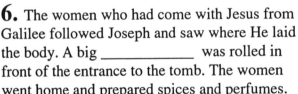

6. The women who had come with Jesus from Galilee followed Joseph and saw where He laid the body. A big _____ was rolled in front of the entrance to the tomb. The women went home and prepared spices and perfumes.

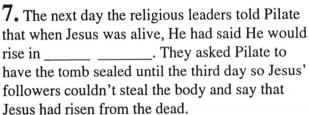

7. The next day the religious leaders told Pilate that when Jesus was alive, He had said He would rise in _____ _____. They asked Pilate to have the tomb sealed until the third day so Jesus' followers couldn't steal the body and say that Jesus had risen from the dead.

8. Pilate said, "Take a _____. Go, make the tomb as secure as you know how." They put a seal on the stone and had the guard stand there watching so that no one could get in or out.

Draw a star in this box when you've read Matthew 27:57-66; Mark 15:42-47; Luke 23:50-56; and John 19:31-42.

Jesus Is Risen!

On the morning of the third day, the women went to Jesus' tomb with some spices, but when they looked inside the tomb, Jesus was gone! Something else that is gone is the last letter of most of the words in the story below. Can you fill in the letters and read the story?

Ver_ earl_ Sunda_ mornin_ Mary Magdalene, Mary th_ mothe_ o_ Jame_, Salome, Joanna, an_ othe_ wome_ wen_ t_ visi_ Jesus' tom_ an_ t_ pu_ mor_ spice_ o_ Hi_ bod_. The_ wer_ wonderin_ ho_ the_ woul_ ge_ th_ gian_ ston_ awa_ fro_ th_ openin_ o_ th_ tom_. Whe_ the_ looke_ u_, the_ sa_ tha_ i_ ha_ alread_ bee_ rolle_ awa_! The_ whe_ the_ looke_ insid_, the_ sa_ tha_ Jesu_' bod_ wa_ gon_!

Th_ wome_ sa_ tw_ angel_ sittin_ wher_ Jesu_' bod_ ha_ bee_. Th_ wome_ wer_ ver_ afrai_, bu_ a_ ange_ sai_, "Don'_ b_ alarme_. Yo_ ar_ lookin_ fo_ Jesu_ th_ Nazaren_, wh_ wa_ crucifie_. H_ ha_ rise_! H_ i_ no_ her_. Se_ th_ plac_ wher_ the_ lai_ Hi_. Bu_ g_, tel_ Hi_ disciple_ an_ Pete_, 'H_ i_ goin_ ahea_ o_ yo_ int_ Galile_. Ther_ yo_ wil_ se_ Hi_, jus_ a_ H_ tol_ yo_.'"

Draw a star in this box when you've read Matthew 28:1-10; Mark 16:1-8; Luke 24:1-12; and John 20:1-18.

Make an 'Eatable' Easter Scene

Easter is when we remember Jesus' resurrection—when He rose from the dead. Now Jesus is in heaven, and if we have faith in Him, we can go to heaven, too! When you make this Easter scene, remember that Jesus is alive!

What You Need

- white Hostess Sno-Ball
- plastic knife
- small paper plate (dessert size)
- flat cookie
- scissors
- toothpick
- tape
- gumdrop
- shredded coconut
- green food color
- colored miniature marshmallows

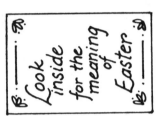

Look inside for the meaning of Easter

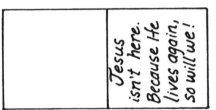

Jesus isn't here. Because He lives again, so will we!

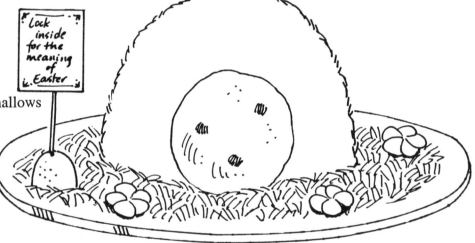

What You Do

1. Cut a hole in the Sno-Ball to make an entrance to the tomb. Be sure that the hole you cut is smaller than the cookie. Scoop out some of the cake and filling and set the "tomb" on the plate. (Be sure to save what you scoop out; you can eat it later!)

2. Now cut out the signs from this page. First tape the one that says "Look inside for the meaning of Easter" to a toothpick, and stick the toothpick into a gumdrop. Then fold the other sign in half and stand it inside the tomb. If it won't fit, hollow out the Sno-Ball a little more.

3. You can make your tomb look like it is in a garden by adding grass and flowers. To make the grass, stir a few drops of green food color into the coconut. Sprinkle the coconut grass around the tomb. Now to make the flowers, slice the marshmallows and put them on the grass in the shape of flowers.

4. Finally, lean the cookie against the tomb so it looks like the stone that sealed it. Have your family and friends look inside to find the meaning of Easter.

Last Week Game

What You Need

- questions cut from pages 39-42
- game board from page 38
- 2 players
- 1 penny
- 1 nickel
- 8 candies of one color for each player (jelly beans, M&Ms, or Smarties work well)
- a pair of dice

How to Play

One player's marker is a nickel and the other's is a penny. Start with both coins on Palm Sunday. Roll the dice and whoever has the highest number is first. That player rolls again, moves the number of spaces on the dice, and does whatever the space says. If you land on a day, answer a question from the question card pile. If you are correct, put a candy on that day and roll again. If your answer is wrong, it is the other player's turn. Continue playing until one of you has a candy of your color on every day of the last week.

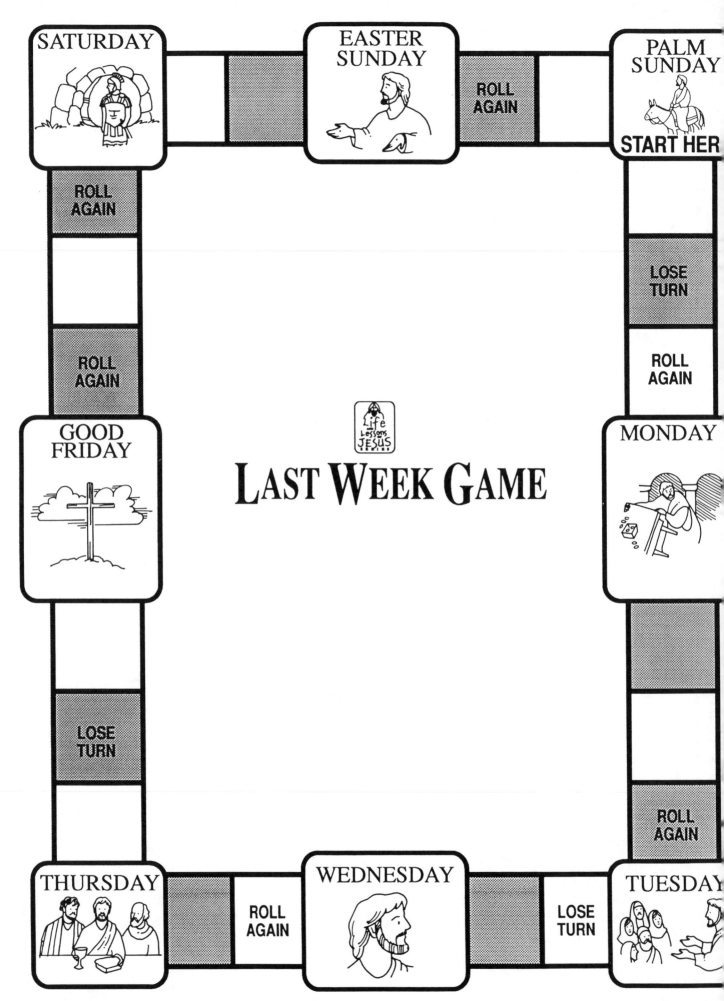

SATURDAY

EASTER SUNDAY

ROLL AGAIN

PALM SUNDAY

START HER[E]

ROLL AGAIN

ROLL AGAIN

LOSE TURN

ROLL AGAIN

GOOD FRIDAY

LAST WEEK GAME

MONDAY

LOSE TURN

ROLL AGAIN

THURSDAY

WEDNESDAY

ROLL AGAIN

LOSE TURN

TUESDAY

LAST WEEK GAME

What city did Jesus enter riding on an animal?

LAST WEEK GAME

What animal did Jesus ride into the city?

LAST WEEK GAME

The city Jesus entered was full of people who had come for which holiday?

LAST WEEK GAME

What word were the people shouting as Jesus entered the city? What did it mean?

LAST WEEK GAME

What two things did people put on the path in front of Jesus?

LAST WEEK GAME

Jesus coming into the city on an animal is called "The Triumphal _____."

LAST WEEK GAME

What did Jesus do to the money changers?

LAST WEEK GAME

What did the religious leaders want to do to Jesus?

LAST WEEK GAME

What did Mary use to wipe Jesus' feet?

LAST WEEK GAME

How much did the religious leaders pay Judas Iscariot?

LAST WEEK GAME

What did Jesus wash at the Last Supper?

LAST WEEK GAME

Jesus wants bread and wine to remind us of what?

3. Passover	2. Donkey	1. Jerusalem
6. Entry	5. Palm branches, clothes	4. Hosanna, save us
9. Her hair	8. Have Him killed	7. Made them leave the temple
12. His body and blood	11. His disciples' feet	10. 30 pieces of silver

LAST WEEK GAME

What did Simon Peter do with his sword in the Garden of Gethsemane?

LAST WEEK GAME

How did Judas Iscariot show the religious leaders which man was Jesus?

LAST WEEK GAME

What did Simon Peter do three times before the rooster crowed?

LAST WEEK GAME

What were the names of the two government leaders who questioned Jesus?

LAST WEEK GAME

What was the crown made of that the soldiers put on Jesus' head?

LAST WEEK GAME

What did the sign on the cross above Jesus' head say? Was it true?

LAST WEEK GAME

Why did Jesus need to die? To take the _____ for our sins because it was the only way we could go to _____.

LAST WEEK GAME

Jesus was buried in whose tomb?

LAST WEEK GAME

Rising from the dead is called what?

LAST WEEK GAME

What do we celebrate at Easter?

LAST WEEK GAME

What day of the week did the women find the tomb empty?

LAST WEEK GAME

Who told the women at the tomb that Jesus had risen?

15. Said he didn't know Jesus

14. Judas kissed Jesus

13. Cut off Malchus's ear

18. This is Jesus, the King of the Jews. Yes.

17. Thorns

16. Pilate, Herod

21. Resurrection

20. Joseph of Arimathea

19. Punishment, heaven

24. An angel

23. Sunday

22. That Jesus rose from the dead and we will, too.

ANSWERS

Page 6
1. Laid us on the ground.
2. Betrayed Jesus.
3. Washed us.
4. His body and blood.
5. He told people he did not know Jesus.
6. Jesus rose from the dead!

Page 8

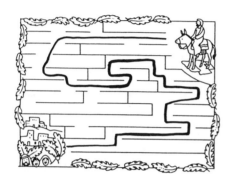

Page 11 The temple was God's house. It was supposed to be a holy place, but the people weren't treating it that way. They sold animals (such as doves) for sacrifices at high prices there. Money changers were there charging way too much. They exchanged foreign money for money that was used in Jerusalem so people could buy animals for sacrifices.

Jesus said, "It is written, 'My house will be called a house of prayer,' but you have made it a 'den of thieves.'" He chased the people who were buying and selling out of the temple. He turned over the tables of the money changers and benches of the people selling pigeons. Jesus wouldn't let anyone come in bringing things to sell.

Every day after that, Jesus taught at the temple. People who couldn't walk or see came to Jesus and He healed them. Children in the temple area shouted, "Hosanna to the Son of David." The Jewish church leaders wanted to kill Jesus because they were afraid people would follow Him instead of them.

Page 12
1. eating, 2. house, 3. dead, 4. Jesus, 5. meal, 6. white, 7. would, 8. money, 9. loving, 10. oil, 11. prophets, 12. kings, 13. hair, 14. Him, 15. others, 16. wasteful, 17. gospel, 18. she, 19. memory

Page 14
1. killed, 2. thirty, 3. silver, 4. supper, 5. dipped, 6. better, 7. born, 8. Garden, 9. kissed, 10. himself

Page 18
1. I am going (to my Father's house) to prepare a place for you.
2. I am the way and the truth and the life. No one comes to the Father except through me.
3. Anyone who has faith in me will do what I have been doing.
4. I will not leave you as orphans; I will come to you.
5. Because I live, you also will live.
6. If anyone loves me, he will obey my teaching.
7. But the counselor, the Holy Spirit, whom the Father will send in my name, will teach you all things and will remind you of everything I have said to you.
8. Peace I leave with you; my peace I give you. I do not give to you as the world gives. Do not let your hearts be troubled and do not be afraid.

Page 20 body, blood

Page 21

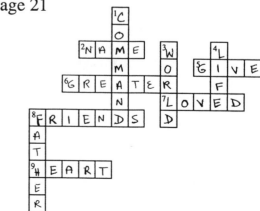

ANSWERS

Page 22   1. garden; 2. Peter; 3. farther; 4. angel; 5. blood; 6. asleep; 7. hour; 8. prayed; 9. resting; 10. sinners

Page 23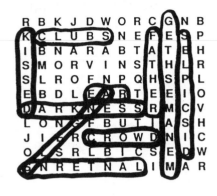

Page 24   Jesus was not guilty.

Page 25   The rooster is hidden beside the woman.

Page 27

Page 31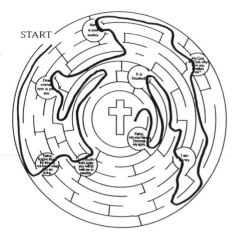

START

Page 34   1. crosses; 2. legs; 3. spear; 4. cloth; 5. tomb; 6. stone; 7. 3 days; 8. guard

Pages 28-29
1. This is Jesus, the King of the Jews.
2. Father, forgive them, for they do not know what they are doing.
3. Jesus, remember me when you come into your kingdom.
4. He saved others, but he can't save himself.

Page 30   Son of God

Page 35   Very early Sunday morning Mary Magdalene, Mary the mother of James, Salome, Joanna, and other women went to visit Jesus' tomb and to put more spices on His body. They were wondering how they would get the giant stone away from the opening of the tomb. When they looked up, they saw that it had already been rolled away! Then when they looked inside, they saw that Jesus' body was gone!

The women saw two angels sitting where Jesus' body had been. The women were very afraid, but an angel said, "Don't be alarmed. You are looking for Jesus the Nazarene, who was crucified. He has risen! He is not here. See the place where they laid Him. But go, tell His disciples and Peter, 'He is going ahead of you into Galilee. There you will see Him, just as He told you.'"

I DID IT!

COMPLETED	DATE	COMPLETED	DATE
☐ Jerusalem, Where Jesus Spent His Last Days	_____	☐ The Mount of Olives	_____
☐ Do You Know About Us?	_____	☐ Prayer in the Garden	_____
☐ The Disciples Find a Donkey	_____	☐ Jesus Is Arrested	_____
☐ Jesus Rides into Jerusalem	_____	☐ Religious Leaders Question Jesus	_____
☐ Hosanna!	_____	☐ Peter and the Rooster	_____
☐ Wave a Palm Branch	_____	☐ Government Leaders Question Jesus	_____
☐ Jesus Clears the Temple	_____	☐ Jesus Is Crucified	_____
☐ Mary Anoints Jesus	_____	☐ Jesus Dies	_____
☐ Make Perfumed Oil	_____	☐ Jesus' Last Words	_____
☐ Judas Betrays Jesus	_____	☐ Make Simple Crosses	_____
☐ The Passover	_____	☐ Why Did Jesus Need to Die?	_____
☐ Washing Feet	_____	☐ Jesus Is Buried	_____
☐ Make Footprints	_____	☐ Jesus Is Risen!	_____
☐ At the Last Supper	_____	☐ Make an Eatable Easter Scene	_____
☐ The Bread and the Cup	_____	☐ Last Week Game	_____

Index of *The Life and Lessons of Jesus* Series